Th

Be Different

A Short Book on Making Permanent Changes

By Martin Meadows

Download Another Book for Free

I want to thank you for buying my book and offer you another book (just as valuable as this one): *Grit: How to Keep Going When You Want to Give Up*, completely free.

Visit the link below to receive it:

http://www.profoundselfimprovement.com/thistime

In *Grit*, I'll tell you exactly how to stick to your goals, using proven methods from peak performers and science.

In addition to getting *Grit*, you'll also have an opportunity to get my new books for free, enter giveaways, and receive other valuable emails from me.

Again, here's the link to sign up:

http://www.profoundselfimprovement.com/thistime

Table of Contents

Prologue

"This time will be different!" Sean proclaimed. He was ready to finally start eating more healthily. He had failed several times before, but this time will be different; he *knows* it will!

His first day goes well. He doesn't feel the temptation to eat a cheeseburger when he passes by his favorite fast food joint. It feels good to drink green tea in place of a diet coke. And his salad tastes like heaven, giving him a foretaste of how bright his future will be.

When he wakes up the next day, a craving for pizza hits him like a brick dropped from a tenth-floor window. But no, he won't eat it. There's no place for pizza in his new diet. As he prepares his breakfast of oatmeal with fruits, he wonders why he had given up so many times before. It's *easy*.

The next few days go without a hitch. Sean doesn't make any exceptions in his nutrition plan and sticks to healthy choices.

And then, on a rainy Monday afternoon, somebody dings his car door at the parking lot. Sean is livid. How could the driver be so reckless? How will he get through the rest of the month now that he needs to pay for the repair? And why is it so cold and gloomy? Couldn't at least the weather be more pleasant? Before he even realizes it, Sean finds himself in his favorite fast food joint, gorging on his favorite cheeseburger (with double fries) and washing it all down with a can (make it two) of diet coke.

Heading back home, Sean is disgusted with himself. How could he have been so rash in his decision to cheat? Was it really worth it to stuff his belly with so much junk food that he had to loosen his belt? He promises himself he won't eat there again. It was just a little slip-up because of that stupid driver. He will soon be back on track. After all, this time is different. He's not going to repeat his past mistakes.

The next day, his boss yells at him for no apparent reason.

Sean desperately fights against the idea of comforting himself with food. He had made a promise to himself to not do that. However, when Sally from accounting suggests that they go grab a pizza for lunch, he finds himself unable to refuse. It's just this one time. Also, Sally doesn't invite him to lunch often. It might be his chance to invite her on a real date.

1500 calories later, with his appetite for unhealthy food reawakened, Sean stops by a supermarket on his way back home. An hour later, he sits in front of the television with a humongous bag of potato chips, which he finishes off before he goes to bed.

When he wakes up the next day, he realizes that he forgot to buy some vegetables and fruits, and two spoons of oatmeal aren't going to cut it for a solid breakfast. From the dark depths of his pantry, he pulls out a half-finished bag of sugary cereals. Oh, there's some chocolate in there, as well. His morning is better already.

At that very moment, unbeknownst to him as he is enjoying a sugar rush, Sean's diet is gone. Over the next couple of weeks, he will be enjoying his old ways to the limit, like a man chugging a bottle of water after finding his way out of the desert.

On a sunny Monday morning, after seeing his old childhood buddy jogging at the local park and looking younger than ever, Sean tells himself, "This time will be different. Let's make a breakfast salad."

It Seems There's No Escape

"This time" is *never* different.

You make some progress, the future is all rainbows and unicorns, and then it isn't. Suddenly you don't even remember why you wanted to introduce this change. What was the point again? *Give up something I enjoy today for some supposed benefits in the future?*

Doing something once is easy. Making a permanent change is hard, and often feels outright impossible.

Except some people are successful at making permanent changes. They stick to their resolutions and their lives *do* get better — permanently.

What makes a difference between those superheroes and mere mortals? And more importantly, can the "mortals" acquire superpowers or should they accept that they'll never be able to permanently change their lives?

I have good news for you: there are no superpowers. Or actually, there are, but they're there for the taking for everybody. They don't require any special inborn abilities except for the willingness to open your mind and learn. True, some people are indeed born with better abilities to handle their appetites, maintain self-discipline, or be persistent in spite of obstacles. However, you can also *learn* these skills.

This short book will equip you with tools to help you seize those superpowers for yourself. This time *can* be different — permanently different.

Before we get to it, though, we need to set some things straight...

First, I'll be the last to say that my process is the only right approach. You can follow it to a T if you want, or you can modify it to suit your situation. Only armchair experts claim that their approach is the only way.

Second, this book is short for a reason. You can fly through it quickly because I don't want to overwhelm you with information. I'll only give you the most relevant information, so you don't get bogged down in unnecessary details. To help you better understand what I'm talking about, throughout the book you'll read some personal stories of mine as well as semi-fictional accounts based on the actual stories of other people.

And finally, in each chapter I'll share some actions with you that you should take in order to implement the advice in your life. Remember that your job is not just to read, but also to *act*. The helpfulness of the advice in this book will depend on whether and (if so) how you implement it.

Now that things are clear, let's focus on the nuts and bolts...

Introducing STAR

Over and over again my readers told me that taking that first step — and then sticking to it — is the hardest part of personal development. Reading books is easy. Most readers know what actions they need to take to accomplish their goals. Yet, they don't do it. STAR is an acronym for a simple process that I designed as a tool to help you overcome inaction.

There are four steps in the process. It starts with the initial shift you need to make to get moving and takes you all the way to the day you reach your goal — and then beyond. Here are the steps:

S — Start. This step goes beyond wishy-washy self-help platitudes and tells you how to introduce a permanent change by linking it with your current lifestyle.

T — Traction. If you feel like you're spinning your wheels all the time and never gaining enough momentum to progress in your journey toward success, this step will give you actionable advice on how to overcome this common problem.

A — Adherence. That's where the real magic happens — and that's also where most people get lost and give up. You need to *earn* success through adherence, and this step will show you how.

R — Refinement. Most self-help advice ends the moment you reach your goal. But in reality, it's only the end of one phase and a beginning of another equally important stage. After all, what's the point of accomplishing a goal, only to fail to maintain your success and revert back to old habits?

If you're tired of consistent unsuccessful attempts and itch for a permanent positive change in your life, let's commence the journey to a better you...

Chapter 1: S Is for Start

Your every action has a reason behind it. While you don't need to know why — specifically, yesterday at 2:37 p.m. — you decided to order a fruit salad instead of a vegetable salad, you *do* need to know why you want to introduce an important change in your life — and what will happen if you don't.

I've talked about motivation extensively in my previous books. I assume you already know about the three different types of motivators: extrinsic, intrinsic, and prosocial.

Just as a quick reminder, extrinsic motivators are about external rewards such as status, money, or praise. They're the weakest type of motivation. Intrinsic motivators are about internal rewards: growth, challenge, enjoyment, or freedom. Prosocial motivation is defined by social psychologist Daniel Baston as the desire to "expend effort to benefit other people.[1]" Intrinsic and prosocial motivators are the most powerful and durable types of motivators.

We won't spend more time talking about finding the right motivation. In all probability, if you are reading this book, you already know *why* you want to implement a change in your life, but you find that this knowledge alone isn't sufficient to help you get started. If you're unsure about how to find the right motivation, please refer to my other books, such as *The Ultimate Focus Strategy*.

In addition to looking for the right *motivators* to do something, you can also look for the negative stimulus, and use that to shake yourself out of inaction. Positive motivation is usually the first — and sometimes the only — tool people use to act on their goals, but often it's not about the thing you want to *get*, but about the thing you want to *escape from*.

How would your future look if you maintained your status quo? Does the vision of things staying the same scare you, or do you feel neutral about it? Is there any kind of pain involved in keeping things as they are? If the perspective of not meeting your goal is painless, your motivation isn't strong enough.

I tried introducing many changes in my life, only to realize I was fooling myself that I cared about making them. I would have understood that I was wasting my time if I had just asked myself if there was any pain involved in not reaching them.

I once wanted to learn French. I researched which specific dialect I wanted to learn and started looking for a teacher. Fortunately, I realized in time that if I hadn't reached my goal of learning French, nothing bad would have happened in my life. There were no negative consequences or pain associated with not learning French, unlike Spanish, which I use often during my travels and can't imagine not being able to speak it.

Don't proceed any further until you imagine the future in which you don't reach your goal. If there's no negative stimulus — no scary vision of things staying the same — you won't implement a permanent change in your life. This is the key teaching of this book. Nothing will change in your life if you don't feel that you *have to* do something about your situation.

EXERCISE #1: MEASURE THE IMPACT OF NOT MAKING A CHANGE

Imagine the future in which you haven't made the change you want to implement in your life. Is it worse? Much worse than today? Or do you feel neutral about it or maybe even realize that not reaching it would lead to a better future?

The negative vision of leaving things as they are has to be intense. Otherwise, you'd find it hard to keep going when you encounter the first obstacles.

If they don't do anything, an obese person who has problems with walking that are due to their excess weight will clearly suffer even more in the future. On the other hand, a person who's fairly lean and healthy probably won't feel a burning desire to develop "six-pack abs," unless they find the prospect of never reaching that goal uncomfortable.

A person who hates their job and feels burned out will probably develop a nervous or physical breakdown if they don't find a new, better job. On the other hand, a person who feels neutral about their job might not be motivated enough unless the pain of remaining complacent or missing out on a better job opportunity is acute.

To produce a lasting shift, once you're sure you deeply care about reaching your goal, we need to focus on…

Motivational Links

When you connect the most important elements of your lifestyle to the change you want to introduce, you'll create what I call a *motivational link*.

Think of it as planning a party. All the usual partygoers know each other well and will feel comfortable at your event.

If you invite a new, shy person to the party, he or she will be more likely to mesh with the crowd — and attend your future parties — if you, as the host, personally introduce him or her to the habitual partygoers and help them find something they have in common.

Now contrast that with an unassisted new attendee, standing awkwardly in the corner of the room, unsure as to who to approach and what to say. How likely will he or she be to appear at your future parties?

The usual partygoers are the existing elements of your life: your personal values, routines, passions, and preferences. The invited shy person is the change you want to introduce into your life.

Make a new change feel welcome with a motivational link, and it will be there at your future parties, too. Force it to awkwardly mingle with people he or she doesn't know, and chances are it will simply leave, never to appear at your parties again.

Let's portray this with an example from my life. For years, I was struggling to get washboard abs. For most people, it generally takes many months, if not years, to reach this goal. Although I consider myself a self-disciplined person, I failed to accomplish it over and over again.

I would start a diet to cut excess body fat and stick to it for a couple of months. Then, after losing 10-20 pounds (5-10 kg), I would realize I was still a long way from reaching my objective. I would get frustrated, take a diet break, tell myself I didn't have enough muscle and go back to my "muscle-building" diet.

Little did I know that all but most-experienced fitness fanatics vastly underestimate how much body fat they need to burn through to uncover their abs. Even if you're relatively lean and fit, this particular fitness goal will test your resolve like no other. Your expectations of how you'll look like after losing 10-20 pounds (5-10 kg) will most likely result in a disappointment.

I *was* motivated to have visible abs. I aspired to feel proud of my body, and it wouldn't hurt that I would look good shirtless. I wanted to further improve my nutritional habits with my fat-loss diet. I also wanted to grow as a person, and considered this difficult physical change a great challenge.

But believe it or not, having visible abs wasn't my biggest ambition in life. As seemingly solid as my motivators were, they weren't sufficiently linked to my lifestyle. Moreover, the pain of *not* having it wasn't strong enough. The fundamental motivators were a good start, but the spark that changed everything was linking my goal to rock climbing, the biggest passion in my life.

Contrary to what you may think, the amount of muscle alone doesn't define the performance of a rock climber. Next to your climbing technique, what matters more is your strength to body-weight ratio. All other things being equal, a climber with a lower weight will perform better than a heavier one.

Even though I was aware of this fact, it still took me many months to put two and two together and realize that developing washboard abs — or rather, lowering my body fat percentage — would also tremendously improve my rock climbing performance. The pain of hampering my progress rate was acute. I didn't want to knowingly improve more slowly because I didn't put in enough effort to lower my body weight. Once I linked my goal with climbing, there was no stopping me. I found the missing piece of the puzzle that made the new change a welcome guest at the party.

Alone, the addition of this single motivational link was enough to help me make a change that I hadn't been able to implement for several years.

Let's work through one more example, and then we'll talk about finding your own motivational links.

Many people struggle to wake up early. They'd love to be like their favorite idols — people who jump out of their beds at 4 a.m. day in and day out, ready to change the world for better. Setting aside the fact that even those superheroes aren't perfect and sometimes sleep in like everyone else, there's only a slight tweak that makes them able to do so: they wake up early because it means they'll get to work on something important to them.

A reader once told me that when she hears the early alarm clock, she realizes she doesn't have anything important to do, so she hits snooze button and goes back to sleep. Two or three hours later, she wakes up at the same hour as always, and the process just repeats the next day.

Let me tell you one thing: waking up early doesn't start with setting your alarm clock at 5 a.m. It starts by figuring out what you're going to do *after* you wake up early. In other words, the new routine needs to be linked to something that is important to you.

If you hate running, you won't jump out of bed to put on your running shoes, while a jogger who absolutely loves running will. An entrepreneur who is working to change the old, stale industry will be in the office by 6 a.m., while a burned-out "9 to 5" worker will barely make it in on time. A twenty-something with no idea what to do with their life would rather sleep than wake up and have to deal with the boredom and frustration of not knowing what to do.

My job as an author is to write on a daily basis. I need to perform this task consistently to provide ever-improving value to you, my dear reader.

I spent years trying to change my night owl routine to that of an early riser. I had some short-term successes, but it wasn't until I discovered that I'm most creative in the early morning that I finally made the change permanent.

I know that when I wake up and perform my early morning routine of writing, I'll count the day as productive — and then I'd be able to spend time doing pleasurable activities guilt-free. This is the first way in which you can build a motivational link — by linking a change with an existing routine.

How to Build Motivational Links With Existing Routines

When I connected early rising with writing, I found it easier to stick to the change because it led to higher productivity in writing — an essential habit that had already been an important part of my everyday routine for a long time.

Linking a change with an existing routine can be something as simple as stacking a new habit on top of an existing one. For example, if you want to learn a new skill, you can link the act of reading a book pertaining to the domain you want to master with a habit of drinking coffee first thing in the morning.

If you have a goal of learning a foreign language, you can link it with your work commute (you can listen to language-learning podcasts), watching TV shows (you can watch them in your target language), or even using your computer (you can switch the language of your browser and favorite sites to your target language). This way, you're learning by immersion, and it all happens almost automatically because you're only tweaking *existing* daily routines slightly.

What do you absolutely *have* to do on a daily basis to feel good? What important habits have you established a long time ago that now feel automatic to you? Answer these questions and you'll identify important routines to which you can link your new change.

How to Build Motivational Links With People-Based Activities

Going to a gym or jogging by yourself takes a lot of willpower. Skipping exercise is more difficult if your regularly jog with a partner who happens to be waiting for you at the front door. This way, you combine something that's always pleasant — hanging out with a friend — with something that may take a couple of weeks before it becomes pleasant — exercise.

Making exercise social is a powerful way to solidify this habit. Studies suggest that exercising with a partner keeps you motivated and accountable,[2] particularly if your workout buddy is slightly better than you at what you are attempting to do.[3]

The positive impact of social support isn't limited just to exercise. You can link all kinds of changes with supportive people.

Dieting is easier if your spouse is on a diet as well, while it's immensely more difficult if they're eating a cake in front of you while your only option for dessert is another serving of broccoli. Including your family in your diet — or at least asking them not to tempt you indirectly — will make dieting less challenging.

Building a business is easier when you have a supportive social circle that is spreading the word about your company or when you join a local business community and grow your company while getting to know new people.

It's easier to put your financial life in order when you learn from other frugal people and exchange ideas with them or offer and receive support when the going gets tough.

Come up with potential allies who can help you introduce a new change. They might be interested in making the change themselves (this will provide the most motivational effect) or they might help you by offering support and acting as your second conscience (such as your spouse not letting you order an unhealthy meal at the restaurant).

You can also link a new change with the positive impact it will have on a person you love.

Grandparents who realize that they need to stop smoking in order to be around their beloved grandchildren for many years to come will have more success in giving up the habit than a person without such a motivation. Obese people who are told they have a high chance of a heart attack within the next year will be more inclined to change their nutrition habits so they won't widow their spouse.

The motivation doesn't have to be that morbid. You can be motivated to save money to support a local non-profit organization that you deeply care about. Or you may remain persistent to finish a difficult project at work so that you can use the accompanying bonus to treat your family with a nice vacation.

I persisted and stuck to my goal of building a successful business for more than 7 years before I finally made a meaningful financial breakthrough because I wanted to help my parents build a house in the countryside. You could have taken all the other motivational links away and I would have still remained determined to make my dream a reality.

When you link the accomplishment of your goal to a positive contribution to the life of a person you deeply care about, you'll have the strongest motivational link there is. Think of people who make you happy or without whom you couldn't imagine your life and link a positive change to them.

How to Build Motivational Links With Passion-Based Activities

Another good way to create a motivational link is to link a change with a personal passion (such as my own example with rock climbing) or something you like doing (even if it's a little thing, such as your addiction to romance novels).

Katherine L. Milkman (from the Wharton School of the University of Pennsylvania, in Philadelphia, Pennsylvania) and her colleagues call this strategy "temptation bundling." They refer to it as: "bundling instantly gratifying but guilt-inducing 'want' experiences with valuable 'should' behaviors providing delayed rewards."[4]

In their experiment, the guilt-inducing "want" experience was listening to page-turner audiobooks while a "should" behavior was exercising. Individuals in the group who worked out while listening to the audiobooks visited the gym more frequently. After the experiment concluded, 61% of them opted to pay to have gym-only access to iPods that contained tempting audiobooks. The experiment suggests that people are more successful at maintaining a positive change if it's accompanied by a "guilty" pleasure — in other words, when they have created a passion-based motivational link.

Note that what researchers refer to as "guilty" pleasures don't actually have to make you feel guilty or harm you in any way.

For example, I love drinking Pu-Erh tea. There's nothing "guilty" about it — it's actually a healthy habit, although I drink the tea primarily for its flavor, not for its health benefits. I linked my early morning routine of writing with drinking Pu-Erh tea to make my mornings even more pleasant.

This additional link makes it even easier to wake up and write because it creates a more all-encompassing experience: there's the freshness of waking up early, silence all around, the rich, earthy taste of Pu-Erh tea, and the satisfaction of words filling the blank page.

Making a new change as pleasurable as possible by combining it with things you like reduces the amount of willpower needed to stick to it, because your reluctance is partly reduced by the prospect of engaging in something you like. Running on a treadmill in a gym? Boring. Jogging in a local park you like being in, while listening to music you love and then drinking your favorite smoothie after you get back home? Much better.

Another way to create a strong motivational link is to find a connection between a passion and the change you want to implement, like I did in my example with rock climbing and developing abs.

For example, let's imagine that you love playing chess and that you're shy, but want to change that. It wouldn't make sense to force yourself to go to a night club to build self-confidence, as this would put you well outside your comfort zone.

Why not join a local chess club and while playing against strangers, develop your social skills and make friends? This would combine an uncomfortable change with something that you're passionate about that's already within your comfort zone.

Don't think of a passion exclusively in terms of a hobby. A passion can be anything that you care about. If you had a billion dollars and would never have to worry about finances anymore, what would you do? How would you ensure that you feel productive?

Answering this question will tell you what you care about so deeply that you could do it without any financial motivation. This will then help you uncover a passion that you can link with your new change.

How to Build Motivational Links With Value-Based Activities

What are your core values in life? What do you prioritize in your life over everything else? When asked about your three top personal principles, what immediately comes to your mind?

Your core values can be things like love, freedom, family, contribution, security, growth, comfort, spirituality, etc. In other words, it's something that defines your life and affects every action you take.

One of my most important motivational links is the link between owning a business and freedom, a core value of mine. I can't imagine my life without the freedom of making money on my own terms, with my own efforts, on my own schedule, through my own choices. Somebody who values stability or teamwork highly might be the complete opposite, and would never imagine a life in which they aren't a part of a big organization.

A person who believes that having strong family ties is the most important thing in the world will be more motivated to work on their side business on the weekends so they can quit their job in the future and dedicate themselves to their family.

A spiritual person can link their resolutions with their faith and the need to live their lifestyle according to their principles.

Identify your core values and link them to the change you want to make. Think about how achieving success will make your life more congruent with your values or how failing to implement this change will keep you from living according to those values.

For example, if you want to save money and comfort is high on your list of core values, think how much more peace of mind you'd have with plenty of savings or how it will feel to be able to switch jobs without financial stress.

EXERCISE #2: CREATE A MOTIVATIONAL LINK

Make a list of people and things like values, passions, or habits that you consider essential in your life. Now that you have your list, come up with potential motivational links.

A burning desire to achieve your goal is a good start, but to produce a permanent shift, it needs to mesh well with other parts of your life.

A simple way to get going is to think of the changes successfully implemented in the past and figuring out how they were linked to the important aspects of your life. If, for example, you gave up smoking because of your children, now you can use the same motivation for a new change, such as improving your diet or finding a better job.

Design at least several motivational links and you'll dramatically improve the chances of making a profound, permanent shift in your life.

S IS FOR START: QUICK RECAP

1. The impact of not making a change has to be negative and intense. If the vision of maintaining the status quo doesn't produce any particularly negative emotions, chances are your goal isn't inspiring enough and you'll find it challenging to keep going when the going gets tough.

2. Creating a motivational link is about linking a change with something important that already exists in your life such as a routine, passion, hobby, important person, or a core value. This way, you reduce the effort and willpower needed to establish a permanent change.

3. Linking a change with a stable routine is about stacking a change on top of an existing habit. The more important your old routine is, and the more you interweave it with the new change, the stronger the motivational link will be.

4. You can link a change with a person you care about through performing a new routine with somebody else (such as exercising with a partner) or finding a person for whom you want to change (such

as losing weight to avoid obesity in your kids). Both approaches provide a powerful motivational boost that can be hard to unleash if you're going it solo.

5. Linking a change with something you like is about finding a way to connect it with something you enjoy, such as listening to a non-fiction audiobook while jogging or combining a new habit of writing 1,000 words a day with drinking a cup of coffee and playing your favorite instrumental music in your headphones.

6. You can also link a change to your core personal values. Identifying how a change can make your life more congruent with your core values — such as how building a business can satisfy your craving for more freedom and autonomy — will help you stick to it in the long term.

Chapter 2: T Is for Traction

Imagine yourself sitting in a 4x4 truck that just got stuck in the mud. As powerful as your machine is, the mud is unforgiving. Your car just won't get out of it, no matter how hard you rev the engine. You have this capable car, the speedometer is showing speed, your wheels are spinning, but you can't get forward momentum.

You lack *traction*.

Finding the right stimulus and developing motivational links are the first steps to introduce a change, but the process doesn't end there. In fact, it's the lack of traction that's the culprit of discouragement and failure.

While sometimes the driver eventually gets out of the tough situation by skillfully operating the car, it often happens that even the best off-road driving expert needs to get out of the vehicle and use a winch to pull the car out of the mud.

And the winch that can get you out of the mud when it comes to personal change is an *identity shift*.

There's No Permanent Shift Without an Identity Shift

As I've already explained in my previous book, *From Failure to Success*, words carry a lot of power. If you look at a problem and tell yourself it's impossible to solve, you probably won't solve it. You'll think of excuses rather than potential solutions. Your brain will use its operating power on a worthless activity.

In his book, *Awaken the Giant Within: How to Take Immediate Control of Your Mental, Emotional, Physical and Financial Destiny*, performance coach and bestselling author Tony Robbins points out that "the drive to preserve the integrity of our own identity is one of the strongest forces in the human personality.[5]"

We feel uneasy to act against our own values or our identities. Hence, committing to a "new you" by choosing the new words by which you'll define yourself will help you gain traction — and to stick to

36

your commitment, in spite of the obstacles you're bound to encounter along the way.

Some of my identities are that of an entrepreneur and an author. If I define myself using these words, this means that I run a business and write regularly. I don't force myself to work on my business or write; it's my identity and the need to stay congruent ensures that I do those things.

I also define myself as a healthy and fit person. This means that I make choices conducive to my well-being. I don't stare at potato chips and cry about how much I'd like to eat them; eating potato chips is *not* a part of my identity.

These aren't mere semantics. If you're a parent, nobody needs to remind you to take care of your children. You're wired this way, and nothing will stand in the way of your earing for your children.

Likewise, if you're an artist, you'll find it impossible *not* to create. The need will always be there, and you won't need a self-help book to motivate you to work on your craft.

This is the power of an identity and you can tap into it whenever you want to, if you follow the simple 2-step process that I'm about to explain.

How Do You Develop an Identity Shift?

Now that you understand why there's no permanent shift without an identity shift, you might be wondering how to actually create one. I call this process CCC: a **C**ommitment, followed by making **C**ongruent **C**hoices.

Step #1: Commitment

You've already created motivational links with your change. This in itself is a great start, but to ensure that your new change will be permanent, you also need to commit to it. There are several levels of commitment:

Level 1: Verbal commitment to yourself

If you're a person who honors self-commitments, making a vow to stick to your change can be sufficient to begin your identity shift.

Please note that the commitment needs to be about a new personal definition, not merely abandoning the old one. If you want to give up smoking, you don't commit to becoming a person who *quit smoking*; you commit to becoming a person who is a *non-smoker*, period. The former implies you still define yourself by the activity you want to give up. The latter means an identity shift.

Also, make sure it's a *specific* commitment and not just a vague resolution that you can adapt to your needs or back out of easily.

"I'm going to become a fit and healthy person who exercises three times a week for at least five hours in total and whose nutrition plan focuses on vegetables, fruits, nuts and whole grains" is a solid, specific commitment, while "I'm fit and eat healthy" is vague. Obviously, with some goals you don't need to be as specific (e,g, there's no point in becoming more specific about what "I'm a non-smoker" means), so use your best judgment.

To turn the commitment into something more tangible than just an idea in your head, create physical reminders of your resolution and surround yourself with them.

When I commenced my plan to shed enough body fat to get visible abs, I created a spreadsheet I called "The Ultimate Cut Plan." Each day, I noted down my weight and calculated weekly averages. Each day, through the act of weighing myself and documenting my progress, I recommitted to my plan. This made my resolution more "real" than simply carrying it in my head.

You can also change your smartphone and computer wallpaper to an image that would represent your commitment, pin relevant photos near your work desk, or set a daily reminder on your phone that reminds you of the commitment you made to yourself. The more reminders you have around you, the stronger your self-promise will be.

Level 2: Verbal commitment to somebody else

Sharing your commitment with a friend will hold you accountable more effectively than a self-promise. The added pressure of another person knowing of your goal will serve as a negative motivator. If you give up, you'll have some explaining to do, and this unpleasant prospect can be sufficient to help you honor your commitment even when the going gets tough.

Share your commitment with a person who's able to offer some tough love when needed and who won't be too lenient. Think of this person as your mentor. You don't want to screw things up and disappoint them. If you couldn't care less about this person's opinion of you, they're not the right person to help you commit to a change.

Please note that merely telling somebody else about a change you want to introduce in your life doesn't actually accomplish anything. Studies warn that people who announce their plans to others are less likely to make them happen because it gives them a premature sense of accomplishment.[6]

That's why you shouldn't go around telling everybody how you're going to change your life. Choose one person and ask them to help you honor your commitment. This is not about happily proclaiming that you're going to run a marathon and expecting standing ovations. It's about asking your friend to kick your ass if you neglect your workout routine or start slipping back into old habits.

Level 3: Commitment contract

The most stringent type of commitment is a commitment contract. Instead of merely proclaiming you're about to change — which often ends up being an empty promise — you design a contract that punishes you when you fail to honor the commitment.

The simplest way to do so would be to give a friend a substantial amount of cash to hold in escrow for a given period of time. I suggest the holding period to last at least several months, so that the change is firmly established in your life.

For example, you can give a friend $1000 (or whatever amount you would consider to be a painful financial loss for you) and instruct them to spend it however they want to if you fail to stick to your diet. If you maintain your diet successfully for a year, you receive your money back. You can also get them to charge you for each slip-up, although you'll need to honestly communicate your failures when they happen.

To make the potential punishment more painful, you can ask a friend to send the money to an organization or political party that you despise if you fail. Warning: this is the most radical and uncomfortable way to commit yourself. While it's extremely powerful, it can also be extremely stressful.

A person opposing oil drilling in the most ecologically vulnerable parts of the world will do whatever they can to avoid sending their money to a group lobbying for more drilling. A Christian will do whatever they can to not send their money to an atheist organization, while an atheist would do whatever in their power to not support a religious organization.

One company that enables online commitment contracts is Stickk.com (that's "stick" with two "k's"). It was created by behavioral economists at Yale University who claim that their methodology can increase people's chances of success by up to 3x.[7] Whether it's 3x or less doesn't matter; the idea in itself *will* reduce your chances of failure and it's worth testing — with or without Stickk. The three founders all successfully used the methodology to instill permanent changes in their lives (their stories are available on the website).[8]

Searching for apps to help you stick to your goals should yield other similar tools to help you with accountability.

No matter which level of commitment you choose, make sure you *do* commit to a change. Merely telling yourself "I'm going to try" doesn't cut it. Commit or don't do it at all.

EXERCISE #3: COMMIT

Choose the level of commitment you'll make to ensure that a new resolution actually turns into a real-world change and not just an empty promise.

Note that you can combine all three types of commitment for an ultimate accountability system.

Step #2: Congruent Choices

A commitment in itself means nothing if it's not followed by real-world actions. Words by themselves have no value for your personal development.

As a popular quote by an unknown person goes, "Commitment means staying loyal to what you said you were going to do, long after the mood you said it in has left you." The way you ensure that loyalty is through congruent choices. Committing to a new change will help you gain traction, but it's congruent choices that will ensure that you actually stop spinning your wheels and stick to your resolutions.

There are two primary tools that will help you make choices that are congruent with your new identity:

1. Self-reflection

You won't make congruent choices if you don't keep tabs on your actions and repeatedly ask yourself whether those actions are aligned with your resolution. This takes constant monitoring and mental presence, but I never said it would be easy as pie, did I?

The simplest self-monitoring tool is to ask yourself regularly — on a daily or weekly basis — if the actions you performed over the last day or week were congruent with your new identity. Imagine yourself as a person with this new identity (or think of a person who possesses this identity) and scrutinize your decisions. Are they aligned with the identity you want to develop?

Take the time to self-reflect and you'll be able to self-correct along the way. Don't do it and you'll unknowingly stray off the path. Think of it as hiking through the wilderness. Isn't it wiser to periodically take a minute or two to check the map or GPS device and ensure you're on the right path than to suddenly realize that you made a wrong turn five hours ago?

If you want to become a fit and strong person, was your decision to forgo exercise because you didn't feel like working out aligned with your new you? Would a person who's fit and strong choose instant gratification over sticking to their promises? Can you imagine Usain Bolt choosing TV over his workout routine because he doesn't feel like doing it?

If you decided to write a book and become an author, would an aspiring writer skip their writing session because they weren't in the mood? Do you think that Stephen King waits weeks for the inspiration to come by his house?

If you want to become an early riser, is your choice to stay up late congruent with your commitment to waking up early? Would an early riser party until the early morning hours or go to sleep no later than at 9 p.m. to ensure a good night's sleep?

Please note that I'm not asking you to overextend yourself. Some reasons to skip a workout (such as being sick or injured) are valid. Then your decision to not exercise isn't a weak excuse; it's still aligned with your resolution. Sometimes making congruent choices means choosing short-term inaction in exchange for long-term sustainability.

Likewise, if there's an emergency, obviously you won't say: "Wait, I need to write this new chapter first." Accomplishing your goals is important, but some things (such as your family, friends, or health) should be more important.

EXERCISE #4: REFLECT

Each evening or at the end of each week, evaluate the previous day or week and ask yourself if your choices reflected your commitment. If not, what should you do from now on to correct your course and get yourself closer to developing your desired identity?

2. Social influence

Social pressure goes both ways. In the traditional, negative sense of this word, people do things they don't necessarily want to do or wouldn't do if it weren't for the crowd. This can often have disastrous effects in children, given how susceptible they are to social pressure. However, adults aren't immune to it, either. While social pressure is generally not a positive thing, we can harness its power to help us make a change.

A 2005 study on social conformity shows that resisting peer pressure causes emotional discomfort.[9] It's difficult, uncomfortable, and mentally draining to have the courage of your convictions. Fitting in feels good, even if you know that mindlessly following the crowd is bad for you.

But what if you found a group that you wanted to join because it exhibited traits and behaviors you'd like to develop in yourself? Whether we call it social pressure or social influence, it could be good for you, even if not completely voluntary.

Imagine that you want to change your eating habits and eat more healthily. The social pressure from which group would help you achieve your goal: couch potatoes or fitness fanatics? If you went to a restaurant with a group of friends and everybody ordered a salad, how much more likely would you be to order a salad than your usual burger and fries? What would you order if everyone ordered something unhealthy?

Again, following the crowd isn't a good idea most of the time, but sometimes the benefits outweigh the cons and can turbocharge your personal shift.

When I started rock climbing and became a part of the local community of climbers, my identity changed without any conscious actions on my part. I also didn't feel pressured into any changes; they happened naturally.

Suddenly I found myself wearing clothes manufactured by outdoor sports brands, using climbing lingo, planning climbing trips, and coordinating my schedule with my climbing workouts.

Inspired by fellow climbers with chiseled physiques, I linked my weight loss goals to climbing performance. I switched my bodybuilding routine to a workout that was more suitable for climbers and general overall fitness, nimbleness and mobility, and now I feel better than ever before.

I also changed as a person. I became friendlier and more relaxed, two traits common in the climbing culture. You can't help but become more social when it's so easy to strike up a conversation with a fellow climber by asking about the conditions on the rock or about the best way to climb a given route.

In addition to that, climbing in itself made me more relaxed and less fearful. Your comfort zone extends greatly if you're essentially risking your life for the fun of it each week. (Even if the risk is actually negligible with proper equipment and safety protocols, your brain doesn't recognize the difference).

My identity changed because of the climbing itself and people with whom I associated. I was influenced by the climbing environment; it wasn't a change I created by myself. However, the changes were good for me. I didn't have to work hard at going through all of these transformations. They happened naturally, as a result of surrounding myself with a specific group of people.

EXERCISE #5: JOIN A GROUP AND LET IT CHANGE YOU

Which group of people exhibits the identity you'd like to develop in yourself? Find a few options, join the one that fits you best, and let it change you.

If you'd like to become a more interesting person, who would help you more: a local chess club or a community of travelers, outdoorsmen, or mountaineers?

If you wanted to build a successful business, would joining a local chamber of commerce help you adopt values, traits, and habits exhibited by successful entrepreneurs?

If you wanted to become an early riser, would it be better to join a local group of joggers who jog in the early morning or hang out with partygoers who go to sleep at 5 a.m.?

Investigate several groups and find out which one best meshes with your personality. You need to feel a desire to become a part of this community, so if you don't agree with all the traits it exhibits, look for a different group that is closer to your core values.

For example, I train in krav maga, an Israeli self-defense system. However, I don't feel particularly connected with the krav maga community because it exhibits some traits I don't feel attracted to; on the other hand, the climbing community (for the most part) fits me like a glove. Both communities could help me become a strong and fit person, but I only let one of them influence me to a larger extent by participating in it more actively.

You can't develop an identity shift overnight and wake up enlightened, but sticking to CCC (Commitment enforced by Congruent Choices) will ensure that, with each passing day, your new identity will imprint itself more and more deeply into your mind and psyche.

Based on my experience, while you can develop new habits in a matter of a few weeks, for a new identity to become a permanent part of your life, you'll need at least several months, if not years.

For example, you can definitely develop a *habit* of waking up early in a month or less, but it most likely won't become a part of your identity until at least several months later. Losing your *habit* of waking up early will make you revert to your old behavior; however, even if you couldn't wake up early for a longer period of time for some reason, once it is firmly established, your new *identity* would eventually make you return to early rising.

When I first switched my daily routine and started waking up early instead of in the early afternoon, skipping a day or two meant losing all progress. It wasn't yet a part of my identity; it was just a habit that I'd been trying to form.

It was only many months later that I finally started defining myself as an early riser, thanks to consistently making congruent choices (and the motivational links we've already discussed).

Today, even if I break my routine of waking up early for a week or longer, I can quickly return to it — something that was impossible in the beginning.

Consequently, CCC is not a magic pill, but it's as close to a silver bullet as you can get. All you need is to follow the rules you established in the beginning and be patient.

Please note that an identity shift usually begins with a new habit, but it's not the habit in itself that redefines you; it's when the habit becomes so natural that you no longer consider it a forced habit and when you don't need any amount of willpower to perform it. Think of it as a habit of drinking coffee or brushing your teeth: you would probably engage in these habits even if it was hard to do so, and that's the level of adaptation you need to change your identity.

Actions, Not Words Reveal If You Really Care

The second step of the STAR process serves as a filter. If you're unable to make congruent choices, despite all the tools we've discussed so far, you probably don't care about your objective enough to continue.

This isn't necessarily a bad thing. It's better to have this realization now and save time rather than waste several months of your life on half-assed efforts and realize it was all for naught.

In his article, "Actions, not words, reveal our real values," successful entrepreneur and blogger Derek

Sivers points out that he's been *talking* about a particular business idea of his for 9 years, but has never launched it.[10] He tried to prove to his coach that he cared about this particular business idea, but in fact he didn't — or he would have already launched it. Derek — an experienced, successful entrepreneur — fooled himself for years, by telling himself he wanted to launch a new business, but his actions proved otherwise.

I use the same filter in my life. One of my strongest allies to help me filter out the wrong objectives is procrastination. Whenever I put off something supposedly important for later, it's usually because I don't care about it enough. My actions — not my words — prove that I'm fooling myself, either by having the wrong goal or not uncovering the right motivations.

For example, I've been thinking about launching a business that would dedicate a portion of its profits to an environmental cause. However, I haven't done anything substantial to make it happen. I only talk and think about it. My actions show that I don't really care about this goal. And it's true — I prefer the free time and flexibility of being a self-published author over new responsibilities as a CEO. I could come up with numerous motivational links and reasons why I *want* to make it happen, but the second step of the STAR process would show that other values are ultimately more important to me. In the end, I'd rather support existing organizations with money I earn as an *author* than to launch a new company purely for this purpose.

Please note that while I was able to filter out this specific goal beforehand, many times before, I had thought that I cared about something, but in the end only realized the contrary after I was a few weeks (or even months) into the process. It can happen to you, too, and that's normal. You won't always know if you really want something until you actually experience what it entails.

That's why it's so important to pause and evaluate your past day or week and ask yourself whether you made congruent choices and whether you're really taking *actions* — and not just saying words — that show that you're committed. If you aren't, maybe it's time to give up, because it's highly probable you aren't pursuing the right goal.

T IS FOR TRACTION: QUICK RECAP

1. There's no permanent shift without an identity shift. If you want to make permanent changes in your life, you need to change your definition of yourself. There's a difference between a person who's "on a diet" and a person who *defines* himself or herself as a fit and healthy individual who is eating whole foods. The former might change in the short term, but it's the latter who will maintain the change permanently.

2. CCC is a 2-step process to develop an identity shift. It starts with a commitment, which is then followed by making congruent choices.

3. There are three levels of commitment; each succeeding level carries increasingly more unpleasant negative consequences if one gives up. Those levels are: verbal commitment to yourself, verbal commitment to somebody else, and a commitment contract in which failure to stick to your resolutions results in a punishment.

4. There are two tools you can use to make congruent choices: self-reflection and social influence. Questioning yourself whether you've made

congruent choices will help you correct any mistakes and ensure that you stick to the plan. Social influence means finding a group of people that exhibit the identity you'd like to possess and letting them influence you; it happens naturally because humans have a tendency to want to fit in.

5. CCC is not a panacea or a magic pill. It will take you at least several months to develop a new identity, but once it's set firmly in place, it will serve you for years to come.

6. Actions, not words, reveal whether you really want to make the change happen. If you struggle to make congruent choices or you constantly procrastinate, you should rethink your objective or your motivations.

Remember that you won't always know in the beginning whether you care about a particular goal sufficiently or not. Until you start the process and directly experience what it feels like to undergo a change, you won't know for sure whether you only like to *talk* about a particular goal or whether you really desire it and your actions prove it.

Chapter 3: A Is for Adherence

Now that we've dealt with the biggest stumbling blocks, it's time for the third step — adherence. Adherence (i.e. the extent to which you're determined to stick to a resolution) is the most powerful filter that separates the successful from the also-rans.

You don't *deserve* a personal change. It's you who has to show that you're worthy of it, and you do *that* through long-term determination and dedication.

Any major positive change offers big rewards, but you need to earn them by persisting through endless tests — the obstacles, failures, and frustrations you'll encounter, have to overcome, push aside and still continue on your journey.

And that's when the third step begins. How do you stay persistent and exhibit grit when the going gets tough? Let's open another toolbox…

5 Tools to Help You Persevere

I'd love to tell you that passing through the third stage of implementing a change will be easy and painless. Unfortunately, in most cases, it's anything but a walk in the park.

Even with the right motivation and commitment, it will still be hard to keep going despite the hardships — which you're guaranteed to experience. Over the years, I've dealt with a fair share of setbacks when implementing changes in my life. Here are the tools I use the most often to ensure that I remain determined to succeed:

1. Imagine the consequences of giving up

When climbing a difficult route, the temptation to give up is sometimes so overpowering that you can't think straight. You know that you're about to fall. You feel how tense your body is. In your stomach, you can almost feel the feeling of falling that you're about to experience . However, letting go right away instead of trying to perform at least one last move before falling means choosing comfort over growth — and this means that you're getting farther away from the change you want to instill in yourself (in this case, becoming a better climber).

Whenever I find myself tempted to back out, I imagine the consequences of giving up. Mind you, it doesn't always work, but oftentimes it helps me grit my teeth and bear the fear for a little while longer.

Recently when I was at the crag, I was wondering whether to climb a route well within my abilities or try a more difficult route that made me feel uneasy.

It would be more comfortable to climb the easier route, but when I imagined the consequences of going the easy way, I chose the harder route. The vision of going home and feeling regret that I hadn't tried a more difficult route was more unpleasant that the discomfort I felt when facing the route itself.

The same happened later on, in a climbing center that I visited in another city. The moment I saw the route, I knew I had to climb it, even though I was frightened just by looking at it. I was shaking by the third bolt and it took me two falls to get to the top, so technically I didn't climb it from the bottom to the top, but it didn't matter. What mattered was that I was driving back home feeling happy that I had faced the challenge head on. I knew that *not* facing the route — even though merely looking at it was as terrifying to me as standing in front of a grizzly bear ready to chew me for breakfast — would in the end be more painful than actually doing it. I can deal with the disappointment of trying and failing, but I find it hard to deal with the fact that I let illogical fear make me back out.

It doesn't matter if you're rock climbing, trying to wake up early, eat more vegetables, build a side business or find a new job — this technique can be used in a variety of situations where a jolt of negative motivation (taking an action to avoid pain) can deliver more punch than positive motivation (taking action to get a pleasant reward).

In the case of my example with climbing, the positive motivation — the potential sense of accomplishment I could get after climbing the difficult, uncomfortable route — was temporarily weaker than motivating myself negatively by imagining the regret of not challenging myself.

EXERCISE #6: FEEL THE PAIN

Whenever positive motivation alone can't help you keep going, think of the negative consequences of giving up. Create a vivid mental picture that will motivate you to do everything in your power to escape it. Here are some questions that will help you feel the pain of giving up and remind you that you don't want it to happen:

1. How would it feel to admit failure to your friends and family? They care about you and your success. Giving up indirectly hurts them as well.

2. How would it feel to admit it to people who criticized your efforts and are only waiting to say "I told you so"? Do you really want to make them happy? Do you really want to see their annoying smirks and feel like a loser?

3. How do you feel now that you've given up and there's no hope for a better future? What about all those dreams of yours that would have come true if you had only persisted?

Now realize that you still have time to prevent this situation and its unpleasant consequences from happening.

Note that when we previously talked about imagining the consequences of not implementing a change (in the first chapter), we performed a similar exercise. When reading the first chapter, if the vision of not accomplishing your goal wasn't particularly painful when you were pondering this question, it will be even harder to keep going when you feel discouraged. After all, if not reaching your goal won't change much about your future, why bother?

2. Remind yourself others are struggling, too

Another good reminder to help you persevere, no matter how hard things get, is to think of people who are struggling and those who struggled before you and converted their struggles into successes. You can find a lot of comfort in reminding yourself that you're not going through anything special — millions before you have done so, millions more are also struggling at this very moment, and millions more will struggle in the future.

It's not what you experience today that matters — it's the long-term process that builds success. In the grand scheme of things, the pain of your current struggles means nothing compared to the benefits you'll get when you succeed. Failures and difficulties are like a rite of passage. It sucks when you experience them, but in the end, you're grateful for the lessons they've given you. Just ask any successful person.

Thinking that others are working on the same goal as you are can also help bring out a competitive spirit and boost your determination. Can you afford to get discouraged or consider giving up while others suck it up and keep putting one foot in front of the other?

For example, I don't generally consider other authors my competition. We collaborate and support each other. However, at the same time, whenever I remind myself that other authors are constantly writing and putting out new books, I feel more compelled to get to work, as well.

This technique will work particularly well if you're a competitive person by nature. I like to think of any difficult moments as big milestones during which a lot of people drop out and only those who truly desire their goal will keep going. You don't want to lose, do you?

3. Look back

When you lose confidence in your ability to persevere, it's easy to lose sight of the fact that you probably overcame similar — if not more difficult — circumstances in the past. Looking back and reminding yourself of those situations can help you remember that there's more power in your tank and you *can* and *will* keep on, just like you did in the past.

EXERCISE #7: LEARN FROM THE PAST

Think of difficult situations in the past that you managed to overcome. How did you handle them? What did you do to push through the obstacles? How did you address the problems that at first seemed insurmountable?

You surely have had more than a fair share of such experiences. They can all serve you. Figure out what you did right back then, and then do it today.

I often talk in my books about putting yourself through voluntary discomfort. That's because I believe that the more experience you have had with uncomfortable situations, the better you'll handle uncomfortable situations in the future, especially when they are unexpected and unplanned.

If you tend to avoid all kinds of discomfort, try to willingly put yourself in some uncomfortable circumstances. It can be as simple as waking up much earlier than you usually do, skipping a meal or two, not spending any amount of money for an entire week, taking a cold shower, or wilderness camping. All of these experiences will help you test your mental resilience and teach you how to tap into your inner strength, grit your teeth, and continue.

I learned a great deal about willpower from my 2-month experiment of taking cold showers daily. I toughened up when I went without food for three days. I developed new ways to cope with discomfort when I fought against my fear of heights by rock climbing, trekking, skydiving, getting on top of the tallest structure in the world as of 2017 (Burj Khalifa), and flying in a hot-air balloon. All of those experiences — and many more — have given me valuable lessons that I use till this day to convince myself that no matter how hard or uncomfortable things get, I can and will keep going.

4. Harness the power of loss aversion

Loss aversion is a concept in decision theory that posits that humans strongly prefer avoiding losses to obtaining equivalent gains.[11] In other words, losing $10 would bring you more unhappiness than winning $10 would bring you satisfaction. The theory goes that humans are hardwired to avoid losses because, in the past, losing a day's food could lead to death while gaining extra food wouldn't contribute to survival in the same life-or-death kind of way.

Loss aversion often leads to illogical decisions. In behavioral science, this is called the sunk cost fallacy: you'll continue investing your time or money into things that no longer make sense, just so you can avoid the pain of loss.[12]

You can use this concept to your benefit, too: remind yourself how much you've already invested in your goal and ask yourself whether you want to lose it all now, just because you feel like giving up. How many sacrifices would go to waste? How much time would be forever lost?

This tool is a variation of imagining the consequences of giving up, but here you focus exclusively on the potential losses to remind yourself of your prior investment and keep going.

Just like any other tool in this chapter, make sure that you're trying to convince yourself to keep going because it makes sense to continue. In other words, avoid throwing good money after bad (I cover the topic of deciding when to give up and when to keep going in more detail in my book *Grit: How to Keep Going When You Want to Give Up*).

5. See the forest for the trees

When things get so hard that you're thinking about giving up, it's easy to get overwhelmed. Suddenly you start wrongly believing that you won't be able to meet the challenge head on or that — this time — the problem you're facing is impossible to solve.

Often the only reason why a problem feels impossible to solve is because you're too close to it.

You won't be able to find a way out until you put some distance between it and yourself. And that's how this last tool works: when you think you've exhausted all of the possible options, take a short break and put some mental and physical distance between you and the problem you're facing.

Going on a short trip or simply not occupying your mind with the goal you've been working on so much recently will help you gain a new perspective. Yes, this means that you'll be losing some momentum for a short period of time, but the rewards will be worth it in the long term because you'll solve the problem more rapidly than if you were to stubbornly stick to it despite being exhausted.

Think of it as resetting yourself. Sometimes an operating system gets so overloaded that it refuses to cooperate. Try as you might, you won't fix it by keeping on. When you perform a simple quick reset, things immediately get back to normal and you can continue working without issues.

A IS FOR ADHERENCE: QUICK RECAP

1. The third step of the process is to earn success. None of us are automatically entitled to get what we desire; we need to prove ourselves by persevering, in spite of difficulties, failure, and discouragement.

2. The first tool you can use to stick to your resolve is to imagine the consequences of giving up. Sometimes positive motivation — imagining the rewards you'll get when you stick to the process — won't be sufficient to keep you going. Negative motivation — visualizing your life after giving up — can provide a kick that will boost your determination.

3. No matter what you're going through, there are other people who are struggling, too. Many people struggled before you and managed to overcome the negative circumstances and reach success.

Remind yourself to focus on the big picture — the daily struggles might be painful, but the long-term outcome will be more than worth them. Consider it a rite of passage you need to go through to get the rewards you crave.

You can also boost your motivation by unleashing your competitive spirit. While you're feeling sorry for yourself, others grit their teeth and keep going. Do you really want to drop out and let them win?

4. Your past experiences can help you handle the current situation. Remind yourself of the difficulties you managed to overcome in the past. How did you do it? What can you learn from those past experiences and apply it today to manage the crisis and keep going?

5. Humans, by nature, will go to great lengths to avoid the pain of loss. Reminding yourself of all the resources you've already invested in your process — time, money, energy, and sacrifices made — will boost your motivation.

6. If you feel overwhelmed and have no idea how to handle the problem you're dealing with, perhaps you need to put some distance between you and the problem to find the right solution. Take a short break, occupy your mind with other matters, and return to the problem when you've rested up. Chances are

you'll approach it with a new perspective and solve it right away.

Chapter 4: R Is for Refinement

You've earned it. A change that was once just a dream is now a permanent part of your life. You feel proud of yourself and how resilient you've been, despite so many obstacles and temptations to give up.

I congratulate you. Few people get to this point, and it's an accomplishment you should celebrate.

However, your work doesn't end here. In fact, it's just a new beginning. The last step makes the difference between truly permanent changes and quasi-permanent wins that slowly (or sometimes rapidly) fade away.

Arthur finally succeeded with his online business. After working so long and so hard on his company, it took off and started generating consistent passive income. He still put in work during the first couple of months after his breakthrough, but then slowly limited the amount of time he spent on his business. After all, income had been consistent for a few months and his business fundaments were stable. It was time to finally start enjoying his newfound freedom.

He packed his things, put them in the trunk of his trusty Toyota, and set off to travel the United States. Life was better than ever before, until one day he woke up to an email communicating that his products had been taken out of the marketplace where he was selling them. His income dropped to zero overnight because he had ignored an important announcement regarding technical updates that he needed to make to his products. It took him a couple of weeks to fix the technical issues and another several months to revive sales.

Arthur achieved quasi-permanent success because he assumed that, after earning his success, it was his to keep forever. He didn't pay enough attention to the changes happening to the marketplace, and he paid for it dearly.

It doesn't have to be this way for you. Embracing the final stage of the STAR process will help you avoid unpleasant hardships and ensure permanent success.

3 Core Principles to Live Your Success

Permanent success is not a right, but a privilege. And it's a privilege limited to those who follow some simple, but essential principles. If you fail to honor this code of conduct, your success may be as fleeting as a shooting star: one moment brightly visible in the sky, and a second later never to be seen again.

Think of celebrities with vast fortunes going bankrupt. Athletes whose performance drops when they sign a lucrative contract and become complacent. Artists who stop creating new music and forever fall off the charts. People who take their physique for granted, forego all the healthy habits that made them lose weight, and regain every single lost pound. Businesses that stop innovating and caring about their clients and lose all their hard-earned business to other companies. People who learned a foreign language, stopped practicing it, and now are struggling to utter a few words in it.

It doesn't have to be this way for you. Here are the most important rules to help you maintain success. Ignore them at your own peril.

1. Keep refining yourself

In his book *The Revolution of Hope: Toward a Humanized Technology*, social philosopher Erich Fromm writes, "What holds true for the individual holds true for a society. It is never static; if it does not grow, it decays; if it does not transcend the status quo for the better, it changes for the worse. Often we, the individual or the people who make up a society, have the illusion we could stand still and not alter the given situation in the one or the other direction. This is one of the most dangerous illusions. The moment we stand still, we begin to decay.[13]"

Over the course of history, stagnation and complacency led countless societies from success to ruin. Once admired, they promptly lost it all when they took their success for granted and deluded themselves it would be there forever.

If there were only one principle to live by to achieve and maintain success, this would be it: you need to keep growing on a daily basis and endlessly improve yourself. Hence, I called the last step of the process *Refinement*.

If you successfully changed your routine and now regularly wake up at 5 a.m., it doesn't mean you can now go to sleep at midnight, thinking that you're so good at getting out of bed early that you can easily wake up early after only 5 hours of sleep.

If you stopped playing video games to build a business and now it's finally successful, it doesn't mean that you can now safely spend entire days playing games. You still need to work on your business to ensure it stays competitive and grows.

If you spent years honing your writing skills and finally released a bestseller, it doesn't mean now you can rest on your laurels and live off your success for the rest of your life (unless your name is J. K. Rowling). You still need to put in work and write more books.

The habits that made you successful are still relevant. Without them, your success will quickly evaporate.

Of course, it doesn't mean that you can never afford to enjoy the fruits of your success. If you love video games, then by all means play them, but don't let them become the primary focus of your life at the expense of your business.

If you successfully lost weight, it doesn't mean you can never again treat yourself to something less than healthy — just make sure it doesn't become a staple in your diet!

If you released a bestseller, by all means take a deserved break from writing and celebrate your success, but eventually you need to resume writing.

In addition to not taking your accomplishments for granted, always think bigger. Set more ambitious goals, improve on top of your past improvements, and strive to always get better.

Just like your body requires constant exercise and new stimuli to stay strong and healthy, success requires new goals and the struggles and challenges that are associated with them.

Keep *earning* your success, and it will remain in your life. Take it for granted, get complacent, forego all of the positive habits you had developed to get where you are, and eventually you'll regret it.

2. Stay humble

One of the biggest dangers that comes with success is the risk of getting too cocky. Fool yourself into thinking that you're the best and, sooner or later, the world will prove you otherwise.

To stay humble means to maintain an attitude that Zen Buddhists call *shoshin* — being open, eager to learn, and free of preconceptions when studying a subject, just like a beginner would — even if you consider yourself an expert. Zen teacher Shunryu Suzuki once wrote: "In the beginner's mind there are many possibilities, in the expert's mind there are few.[14]"

Assuming that you already know everything you need to know will close your mind to new learning opportunities and hinder your growth. Consequently, never let your success make you believe you know it all. This comes down to remaining vigilant of your thoughts, staying open to new ideas, and constantly reminding yourself that your accomplishments don't automatically make you superior to others.

I like to stay grounded by helping people who are working on the goals I've already reached. This practice makes me relive my past struggles, learn something new by sharing my knowledge, and exposes me to new ways of thinking — all of which help me stay humble. Speaking of which, the third principle for living your success is to…

3. Pay it forward

You don't achieve success in a vacuum. There are always other people involved, even if you've never met them or they'll never know how much they've helped you.

I know that if it weren't for several people who had freely shared their own experience about book publishing, I wouldn't be where I am today.

If it weren't for some entrepreneurs who offered me advice through their books, emails, or personal messages, I would have been less likely to become a successful businessman. I wouldn't be able to support myself by writing books if it weren't for people like you, my dear reader.

And that's just the tip of the iceberg. Somebody invented and commercialized the Internet. I benefit from the promotional power of online book retailers. I learned how to write, thanks to books written by other authors. Going way back, it all started with my parents, who provided a roof over my head, food, education, safety, and fulfilled numerous other needs when I was growing up.

You won't be always able to give back to the people who helped you, but you can always pay it forward. Helping others — or supporting any worthy cause — is one of the most rewarding feelings in the universe, and it makes the world a better place at the same time.

Every accomplishment generates resources you can extend to others — and it doesn't have to be money. For example, whenever you accomplish a new goal, you become an expert in how to reach it. To a person struggling to reach their goals, this knowledge is more valuable than any amount of money. Other resources you gain through your successes include things like:

- your free time. When you build a successful business that operates without your involvement, you can spend your free time coaching promising entrepreneurs or leading a local kid's sports team.

- your connections. If you found your dream job thanks to consistent networking, you can reach out to the same network to help your qualified friends get the job they desire.

- your best self. Achieving success in any area of life makes you more confident, fulfilled, and happier. You can extend these positive emotions to other people in your life.

Living by this principle provides inspiration to keep improving and gives meaning to your accomplishments because they become about more than just you.

At some point, you won't gain additional satisfaction from another pound lost. Your body will be as you wish it to be. However, you'll always feel fulfilled when you share your knowledge with others and help them get into shape.

At some point, more money in your bank account will no longer provide such a rewarding feeling as it did in the past. However, you'll always feel motivated to work to extend financial support to causes you care about.

At some point, you'll no longer feel that waking up early in the morning, eating healthy, or exercising regularly is something special. However, to people who will listen to your advice and transform their daily routines, it will make a world of difference.

No matter your accomplishments, becoming more successful generates more success — not only for you, but also for other people. Pay it forward, and you'll consistently make the pie bigger for everyone — including you.

R IS FOR REFINEMENT: QUICK RECAP

1. Success is not a given. You can't rest on your laurels when you finally become successful because it will hinder your growth and eventually take away the things you had worked so hard to achieve.

2. The first core principle for living your success is to keep earning it. Resist the temptation to think that when you achieve success, you have a license to get lazy and stop growing. Always think bigger, and ensure that success stays in your life by setting new goals, experiencing new struggles, and becoming a better and better person.

3. The second principle is to stay humble. Cockiness leads to a closed mind, and closing your mind to new ideas limits your growth. No matter how successful you are, the world can always remind you — often in a painful way — that you aren't superior to others.

4. The third principle is to pay it forward. You didn't achieve your success in a vacuum. It happened because of other people who provided you with

knowledge, tools, social support, or extended a helping hand in a different way. Remain inspired to grow more by helping others and supporting causes you believe in — whether financially, or with your knowledge, connections, free time or other resources.

Epilogue

I promised you a short read with the intention of giving you as much applicable information as quickly as possible, so now it's time to say goodbye.

However, before we part ways, I want to tell you how much I appreciate you reading this book. I often talk with people interested in making new personal changes or accomplishing big goals. Unfortunately, they rarely do anything but talk, and it pains me a great deal to see so much wasted potential.

You belong to a small minority of people who don't merely talk, but also *do* something about their dreams. Finishing this book — something most readers don't do even with books as short as this one — means that you're committed to changing yourself.

Now is the time for you to take the next step: *prove* you're committed and *become* the change you crave so much.

You've already demonstrated some level of dedication; I urge you to keep the momentum going and take real-world actions. Personal growth is an immensely rewarding undertaking. What you learn and experience through your own efforts will be infinitely more valuable, satisfying, and life-changing than what you now know in theory.

In his book, *How to Stop Worrying and Start Living*, Dale Carnegie (one of the most legendary personal development authors) wrote the following thought: "Every day is a new life to a wise man."

I know that you're wise, because only wise people spend time on education. Isn't it time for *you* to begin a new life, too?

Download Another Book for Free

I want to thank you for buying my book and offer you another book (just as valuable as this one): *Grit: How to Keep Going When You Want to Give Up*, completely free.

Visit the link below to receive it:

http://www.profoundselfimprovement.com/thistime

In *Grit*, I'll tell you exactly how to stick to your goals, using proven methods from peak performers and science.

In addition to getting *Grit*, you'll also have an opportunity to get my new books for free, enter giveaways, and receive other valuable emails from me.

Again, here's the link to sign up:

http://www.profoundselfimprovement.com/thistime

Could You Help?

I'd love to hear your opinion about my book. In the world of book publishing, there are few things more valuable than honest reviews from a wide variety of readers.

Your review will help other readers find out whether my book is for them. It will also help me reach more readers by increasing the visibility of my book.

About Martin Meadows

Martin Meadows is the pen name of an author who has dedicated his life to personal growth. He constantly reinvents himself by making drastic changes in his life.

Over the years, he has regularly fasted for more than 40 hours, taught himself two foreign languages, lost more than 30 pounds in 12 weeks, run several businesses in various industries, took ice-cold showers and baths, lived on a small tropical island in a foreign country for several months, and wrote a 400-page novel's worth of short stories in one month.

But self-torture is not his passion. Martin likes to test his boundaries to discover how far his comfort zone goes.

His findings (based both on his personal experience and scientific studies) help him improve his life. If you're interested in pushing your limits and learning how to become the best version of yourself, you'll love Martin's works.

You can read his books here:

http://www.amazon.com/author/martinmeadows.

[1] Batson, C. D. (1987). Prosocial motivation: Is it ever truly altruistic? In L. Berkowitz (Ed.), *Advances in experimental social psychology* (Vol. 20, pp. 65–122). New York: Academic Press.

[2] Irwin, B. C., Scorniaenchi, J., Kerr, N. L., Eisenmann, J. C., & Feltz, D. L. (2012). Aerobic exercise is promoted when individual performance affects the group: a test of the Kohler motivation gain effect. *Annals of Behavioral Medicine: a Publication of the Society of Behavioral Medicine*, 44(2): 151–9. doi: 10.1007/s12160-012-9367-4.

[3] Feltz, D. L., Irwin, B. C., & Kerr, N. (2012). Two-player partnered exergame for obesity prevention: using discrepancy in players' abilities as a strategy to motivate physical activity. *Journal of Diabetes Science and Technology*, 6(4): 820–7. doi: 10.1177/193229681200600413.

[4] Milkman, K. L., Minson, J. A., & Volpp, K. G. M. (2013). Holding the Hunger Games Hostage at the Gym: An Evaluation of Temptation Bundling. *Management Science*, 283–299. doi: 10.1287/mnsc.2013.1784.

[5] Robbins, T. (1991). *Awaken the Giant Within: How to Take Immediate Control of Your Mental, Emotional, Physical and Financial Destiny*. Free Press.

[6] Gollwitzer, P. M., Sheeran, P., Michalski, V., & Seifert, A. E. (2009). When Intentions Go Public. Does Social Reality Widen the Intention-Behavior Gap? *Psychological Science*, 20(5): 612–618. doi: 0.1111/j.1467-9280.2009.02336.x.

[7] FAQ - About stickK. Retrieved June 11, 2017 from https://www.stickk.com/faq/about/About+stickK.

[8] https://www.stickk.com/founders.

[9] Berns, G. S., Chappelow, J., Zink, C. F., Pagnoni, G., Martin-Skurski, M. E., & Richards, J. (2005). Neurobiological correlates of social conformity and independence during mental rotation. *Biological Psychiatry*, 58(3): 245–253. doi: 10.1016/j.biopsych.2005.04.012.

[10] Sivers, D. (2017, June 16). Actions, not words, reveal our real values. Retrieved June 16, 2017 from https://sivers.org/arv.

[11] Kahneman, D. & Tversky, A. (1992). Advances in prospect theory: Cumulative representation of uncertainty. *Journal of Risk and Uncertainty*, 5(4): 297–323. doi: 10.1007/BF00122574.

[12] Arkes, H., & Blumer, C. (1985). The Psychology of Sunk Cost. *Organizational Behavior and Human Decision Process*, 35: 124–140. doi:10.1016/0749-5978(85)90049-4.

[13] Fromm, E. (1968). *The Revolution of Hope: Toward a Humanized Technology*. HarperCollins.

[14] Suzuki, S. (1970). *Zen Mind, Beginner's Mind.*

Made in the USA
Middletown, DE
09 March 2018